DATE DUE

Simon, Mary Manz
Stop! It's Christmas

DEMCO

STOP! It's Christmas

Mary Manz Simon
Illustrated by Rick Incrocci

SAINT LOUIS

Books by Mary Manz Simon from Concordia Publishing House

Hear Me Read Level 1 Series
What Next?
Drip Drop
Jibber Jabber
Hide the Baby
Toot! Toot!
Bing!
Whoops!
Send a Baby
A Silent Night
Follow That Star
Row the Boat
Rumble, Rumble
Who Will Help?
Sit Down
Come to Jesus
Too Tall, Too Small
Hurry, Hurry!

Hear Me Read Level 2 Series
The No-Go King
Hurray for the Lord's Army!
The Hide-and-Seek Prince
Daniel and the Tattletales
The First Christmas
Through the Roof
A Walk on the Waves
Thank You Jesus

Little Visits on the Go
Little Visits for Toddlers
Little Visits with Jesus
Little Visits Every Day

God's Children Pray
My First Diary

Published by Concordia Publishing House
3558 S. Jefferson Avenue, St. Louis, MO 63118-3968
Manufactured in the United States of America

3 4 5 6 7 8 9 10   06 05 04 03 02 01 00 99 98

Brian watched everything. Mrs. Kirby untangled
Christmas lights. Mr. Kirby climbed a ladder to hang them.
Skippy—the Kirby's little dog—ran around in circles and
jumped into a box. He couldn't get out! Brian laughed.

Bang! Bang! Bang!
Mr. Kirby hammered a sign into the ground. It was the last decoration.

Why is Mr. Kirby putting that sign in front of his house? Brian wondered. Brian could read the word *Stop*, but this sign had more words. And stop signs belonged near the street.

"Sarah, Sarah!" Brian tugged at his sister's sleeve. He pointed to the sign across the street. "What does that say?"

Sarah put her hand over the phone. "It says, 'Santa Stops Here,'" she whispered. Then she went back to her conversation.

Brian walked back to the window. "Santa stops here," he said to himself. No one at his house ever talked about Santa.

If Santa visited Mr. and Mrs. Kirby, would he come to Brian's house too?

Just then Brian heard the front door open. "Dad!" he yelled. Brian held the door open as his dad came in, his arms full of Christmas packages. "Dad, will Santa stop at our house this year?" he asked.

"No," Dad said. "We don't really need Santa with all these presents."

Brian ran upstairs to find Ashley, his biggest sister.
"Ashley," he asked. "Will Santa stop at our house?"

Ashley put down her book and smiled at him. "Probably not," Ashley said. "We don't need him for our Christmas."

Brian ran downstairs. "Mom!" he called. "Mom?"
"I'm in the kitchen, Brian," Mom answered. She set a
bowl of frosting by the big cake she had made.

"Mom," Brian asked. "Will Santa stop at our house
this year?"

"I don't think so," said his mom.

"The Kirbys have a sign for Santa. Santa is going to stop at their house. Why can't he come here too?" Brian wanted to know.

Mom stopped frosting the cake and smiled at Brian. "Because we celebrate Jesus' birthday. That's what Christmas is. We don't need Santa to remind us that Jesus is in our hearts," she explained.

"Couldn't Santa stop at our house and bring just *one* present? Just one present for me?" Brian asked.

"Well," his mother said slowly, "I'm not sure we need Santa. The idea of Santa came from a kind man named St. Nicholas who lived in Holland long ago. Nicholas gave gifts to poor people. Some people think that Santa—or St. Nicholas—is the most important thing about Christmas. But we know Christmas is the day we celebrate baby Jesus' birthday."

"And Christmas Eve is so busy," Mom explained.
"Aunt Dorothy and Uncle Jerry come over for supper, and
then we go to church."

"I like that," said Brian. "Especially when we light candles and sing."

Mom continued, "And when we get home from church, Dad starts a fire in the fireplace. Then we open the presents in our stockings."

"That's fun too," Brian said.

"And then—on Christmas morning—Dad reads the story about baby Jesus being born."

"And I get to put Jesus in the manger under the tree," Brian reminded her.

"Yes, that's your job," Mom smiled. "Then we open the rest of our presents. And after dinner we sing 'Happy Birthday to Jesus.'"

"And we blow out all the candles!" Brian said. "I love Christmas!"

"Some boys and girls believe Santa is real," Mom explained. "One of the things we can do is tell them the real reason for Christmas is Jesus."

Brian thought about that. The air around him seemed to be full of hugs—all because Jesus was born.

Brian wandered back to the family room and looked out the window. There was the sign—Santa Stops Here. Brian was quiet, just thinking. Mom and Dad always said Jesus loved him so much that He gave His life for him. He liked sharing the love of Jesus. That's what made Christmas special.

Then Brian had an idea!

Brian dashed upstairs. He opened his closet and pulled out a big sheet of paper and some markers. He ran to Sarah's room.

"Sarah, Sarah," he gasped, out of breath, "help me."
Sarah spelled some words for him and helped him cut the
paper. Brian ran back to his room and found a red marker.
He colored and colored.

There! It was perfect. Mom was right. Santa didn't have to stop at their house.

Brian raced to the family room. He squiggled underneath the tree. His sign needed to be at the manger.

Brian sat back. "Jesus Stops Here," he read. Brian knew he would have a very merry Christmas.